VICTOR SHEV

My First Book of Rhythm

A Comprehensive Workbook
for developing Sense of Music Pulse,
Rhythm and Sight-reading Skills.

- Part One -

ILLUSTRATIONS BY
VERONIKA BEKKER
MARIA DAMGAARD

My First Book of Rhythm
Part one

ISBN 978-0-9917624-8-4

© Victor Shevtsov, 2014
© VITTA Music Library For Children
  All rights reserved.

Any duplication, adaptation or arrangement of the materials contained in this book requires the written consent of the Publisher.

Unauthorized photocopying is prohibited.

Printed in Canada

Foreword

Teaching students to read and play different rhythms can be ineffective if their sense of musical pulse and rhythm is not well developed. Theoretical explanations of note values, time signatures, and strong and weak beats are certainly indispensable; however, it is not less important in training beginners to include exercises that will help them develop their sense of rhythm.

Rhythm and rhythmic pulse do not pertain to music only. It is also characteristic of speech and different types of (motor) movements such as walking, running, marching, and dancing.

Children's play activities show that they all have a good sense of rhythm. It is obvious to anyone that has observed how children recite rhymes, march, rock their dolls or skip a rope.

The reason that a music instructor may encounter certain difficulties in teaching students to read and understand musical rhythms is usually not their lack of sense of rhythm; rather, it is the inability of young children to correlate it with the way we write music.

The exercises in "My First Book of Rhythm" are intended to bridge the gap between children's habitual rhythmic activities and the principles of writing the rhythm in music. They are based on close analogies that are found between rhythm of speech and rhythm of music, the length of the words and note values or length of the music bars, stresses in the words and strong and weak beats in music, etc.

For these exercises we use simple children's rhymes, short phrases and simple words of different length and phonetic structure. Reciting, clapping and counting such speech patterns help children little by little to correlate them with the ideas of regular musical pulse, different note values, music bars, strong and weak beats, and so on. After such exercises the process of learning to read musical rhythm goes much smoother.

In each chapter of the book, one aspect of the rhythm is explored. "My First Book of Rhythm, Part One" is focused on musical pulse, the length of musical sounds and different note and rest values (up to eighth notes and including dotted quarters), and the bar structure of music.

In "My First Book of Rhythm, Part Two", students will study new note values including triplets, new time signatures, strong and weak beats, incomplete bars, and ties.

More complicated rhythmic devices, such as polyrhythmic structures and syncopations, are explored in "My First Book of Rhythm, Part Three".

Sincerely,
Victor Shevtsov

Table of Contents

I. Music Pulse 5

II. Short and Long Sounds 12

III. Beats and Counts. Note Values. 17

IV. Bars. Bar Lines. Time Signature 34

V. Note Values. Dotted Half Note 39

VI. Rests 43

VII. Note Values. Eighth Notes 49

VIII. Rests. Eighth Rests 60

IX. Overview Exercises 70

I. Music Pulse

Music can be fast and slow. The pace or speed of music is called the Tempo. When listening to music we can also feel its Pulse. It is similar to the pulse, that we feel when we walk, march or recite rhymes.

1 Recite the following rhymes and clap evenly at a **Moderate Pace**. One word = one clap.

Rain, rain, all day, rain, rain, all May.

Night, day, night, day, rain, rain, all May.

Bill, Bill, sit still. Kate, Kate, stand straight.

Nick, Nick, be quick. Bob, Bob, please stop.

Walk, walk, don't talk. Look, look – black rook.

Two, one, two, one, two stars – one sun.

© Victor Shevtsov, 2014

2 Recite and clap evenly at a **Moderate Pace**.
One clap for every word.

One, two, one, two, two feet, one shoe.

Three, four, three, four, three floors, one door.

Five, six, five, six, one hen, five chicks.

Nine, ten, nine, ten, nine men, one pen.

Ten, nine, ten, nine, ten cakes all mine.

Nine, eight, nine, eight, nine skis, one skate.

Six, five, six, five, six bees, one hive.

Four, three, four, three, four birds one tree.

3 Recite the following rhymes and clap evenly at a **Fast Pace**. Make one clap for each word.

Hop, hop, don't stop. Run, run – it's fun.

Jump, leap, spring, skip. Be fast, don't slip.

Green frogs, grey frogs, blue frogs like bogs.

Dark bogs, light bogs, all frogs like bogs.

White, black, white, black, I lost my snack.

Black, white, black, white, I like your kite.

Black cats chase mice, they don't eat rice.

White cats chase rats, they don't eat bats.

4 Recite the following rhymes and clap evenly at a **Slow Pace**. Make one clap for each word.

👏 👏 👏 👏 👏 👏 👏 👏
Two crocs, two crocs loved long, long walks.

👏 👏 👏 👏 👏 👏 👏 👏
They walked all day a long, long way.

👏 👏 👏 👏 👏 👏 👏 👏
Don't run, don't trot, it's hot, too hot.

👏 👏 👏 👏 👏 👏 👏 👏
Just walk or stroll, don't rush at all.

👏 👏 👏 👏 👏 👏 👏 👏
Aunt Grace, Aunt Grace wears nice, white lace.

👏 👏 👏 👏 👏 👏 👏 👏
She does her walks in long, white socks.

👏 👏 👏 👏 👏 👏 👏 👏
Aunt Jane, hates rains and lives in Spain.

👏 👏 👏 👏 👏 👏 👏 👏
She hates the planes and goes by train.

Recite the following rhymes while marching evenly at a **Moderate Pace**. One word = one step.

One, two, two, one, strong legs are fun.
Short legs can run, one two, two, one.
Long legs have won, one, two, two, one.
Short legs, long legs, quick legs are fun!

Six, five, four, three, Jane drinks black tea.
One day black tea, one day green tea,
One day white tea, six, five, four, three.

Two, one, one, two, Bob likes beef stew.
Two, one, one, two, I like it too.
Two, one, one, two, John likes fish stew.
Two, one, one, two, I like it too.

Three, two, two, three, I like to ski.
Eight, nine, nine, eight, Jack likes to skate.
Five, six, six, five, Kate likes to dive.

6 Recite the following rhymes while clapping and marching at the same time. One word = one step.

Moderate speed

Six,   five,   five,   six,   Grace   knows   all   tricks.
One,   two,   three,   four,   Tom   likes   to   score.
Four,   three,   two,   one,   Ann   likes   to   run.

Nine,   ten,   ten,   nine,   ten   cones,   one   pine.
Ten,   nine,   nine,   ten,   nine   ducks,   one   hen.
Eight,   nine,   nine,   eight,   nine   spoons,   one   plate.

March and clap a little faster

I   had   just   once   a   chance   to   dance,
But   baked   two   times   a   cake   from   rice.
Three   times   I   ate   full   plate   of   dates,
And   drank   four   times   my   tea   with   limes.

Six   times   I   won   a   hot   cross   bun,
But   lost   eight   times   one   of   my   dimes.
I   watched   nine   times   how   Big   Ben   chimes,
And   heard   ten   times   my   Mom   say   rhymes.

10

7 Recite the following rhymes alternating marching and clapping. Keep **moderate speed.**

 Green, blue, white red, I like rye bread.

 Green, blue, red, white, my shoes are tight.

 Pink, brown, grey, black, I ate my snack.

 Pink, brown, black, grey, we sail all day.

 Grey, black, brown, pink, my boat won't sink.

 White, blue, pink, rose, I have ten toes.

 White, blue, rose, pink, I spilled some ink.

 Grey, black, pink, brown, I lost my gown.

 My dog and cat, they like to chat.

 My cat and dog, they like to jog.

 My dear pet bear has dark brown hair.

 If whales could be as small as snails,
Then snails could eat for lunch fresh whales.

II. Short and Long Sounds

Music sounds are similar to the words in our speech, and like words, they can be short and long.

1 Learn to clap and recite short words at a **fast pace**.
Each word is only **one syllable (part)**. One word = one clap.

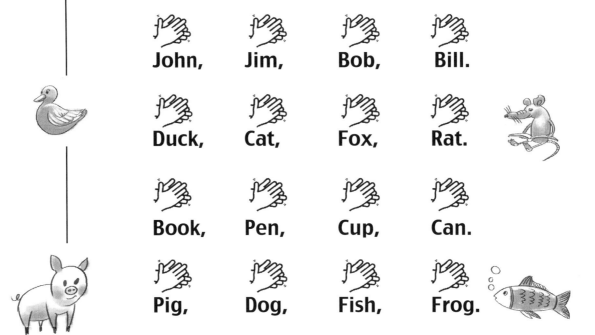

John,   Jim,   Bob,   Bill.

Duck,   Cat,   Fox,   Rat.

Book,   Pen,   Cup,   Can.

Pig,   Dog,   Fish,   Frog.

2 Learn to clap and recite longer, **two - syllable** words.
Make one clap for each word. Distinctly pronounce each syllable.

Ja – son,   Chris – ty,   An – drew,   Bran – don.

Ti – ger,   Lob – ster,   Don – key,   Mon – key.

Pum – pkin,   Pep – per,   Egg – plant,   Mush – room.

Pia – no,   Trum – pet,   Win – dow,   Bas – ket.

3 Learn to clap and recite long, **three - syllable** words.
Make one clap for one word. Pronounce clearly every syllable.

Black-ber-ry, **Rasp**-ber-ry, **Straw**-ber-ry, **Blue**-ber-ry.

Cu-cum-ber, **Broc**-co-li, **Pep**-per-mint, **Ce**-le-ry.

Oc-to-pus, **Cro**-co-dile, **E**-le-phant, **Di**-no-saur.

Grass-hop-per, **But** – ter-fly, **La** – dy-bird, **Dra**-gon-fly.

4 Learn to clap and recite super long, **four - syllable** words. Make one clap for each word. Recite at a **fast pace**. Pronounce clearly every syllable.

He – li – cop – ter,   **Cat** – ter – pil – ler.

Wa – ter – me – lon,   **Cau** – li – flow – er.

Cal – cu – la – tor,   **Al** – li – ga – tor.

Ex – pla – na – tion,   **In** – for – ma – tion.

5 Learn to clap and recite patterns with short, **one - syllable** words and longer, **two - syllable** words. Pronounce evenly and clearly every syllable. Recite **at a fast pace.**

Duck, **Duck,** **Duck** – ling.

Pen, **Pen,** **Pen** – cil.

Book, **Book,** **Book** – case.

Pig, **Pig,** **Pig** – let.

6 Learn to clap and recite patterns with short, **one - syllable** words and long, **three - syllable** words. Maintain **a lively pace.**

Cuke, **Cuke,** **Cuke,** **Cu** – cum – ber.

Grass, **Grass,** **Grass,** **Grass** – hop – per.

Croc, **Croc,** **Croc,** **Cro** – co – dile.

News, **News,** **News,** **News** – pa – per.

7 Learn to clap and recite patterns with short **one - syllable** words and super long **four - syllable** words. Maintain **a lively pace**.

Sit, Sit, Sit, Sit, Ba – by – sit - ter.

Pick, Pick, Pick, Pick, Pic – nic – bas – ket.

Fly, Fly, Fly, Fly, He – li – cop – ter.

Boys, Girls, Boys, Girls, Kin – der – gar – ten.

8 Learn to clap and recite patterns with **two - syllable** words and **four - syllable** words.

Birth – day, Birth – day, Birth – day – par – ty.

Wa – ter, Wa – ter, Wa – ter – me – lon.

Pe – per, Pe – per, Pe – pe – ro – ny.

Mar – ket, Mar – ket, Su – per – mar – ket.

9 Learn to clap and recite patterns with **one - syllable, two - syllable** and **three - syllable** words. Recite evenly every syllable.

👏	👏	👏
Wash,	**Di** – shes,	**Dish** – wash – er.
Sun,	**Sun** – roof,	**Sun** – flo – wer.
Sky,	**Sky** – train,	**Sky** – scra – per.
Eyes,	**Eye** – brows,	**Eye** – glas – ses.

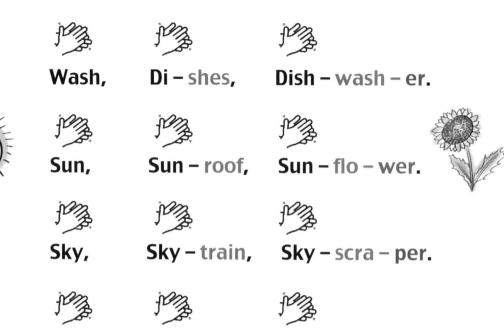

10 Learn to clap and recite patterns with **one - syllable, two - syllable** and **four - syllable** words. Maintain **a fast pace**.

👏	👏	👏
Hot,	**Pep** – per,	**Pep** – pe – ro – ny.
Sweet,	**Wa** – ter,	**Wa** – ter – me – lon.
Flow,	**Flo** – wer,	**Cau** – li - flo – wer.
Fly,	**High** – er,	**He** – li - cop – ter.

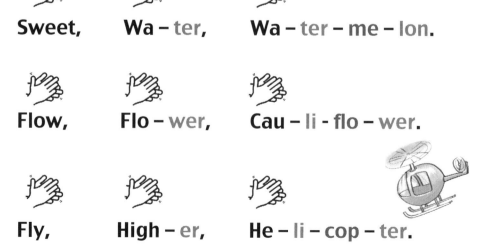

III. Beats and Counts • Note Values

- Music sounds, like words can be short and long.
- We measure the length of words by the number of syllables.
- We measure duration of music sounds by **counts** or **beats**.

1 Learn to clap and count short, one syllable words: one word = one clap; one count = one clap.

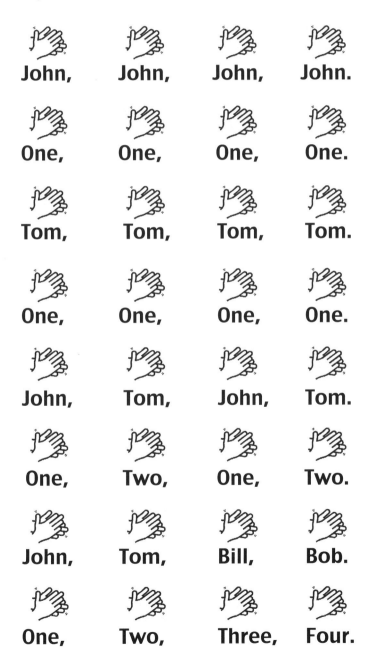

© Victor Shevtsov, 2014

4 Find your own words to recite with Quarter Notes.
One note = one clap. One count for each quarter note.

- Clap and recite what you see on the pictures.
- Clap and count out loud: **one, two, three, four.**

Vocabulary

whale
shark
fly
sheep
ant
wolf
fox
sheep
crab
pawn
fork
plate
cup
knife
book
car
bike
stick
train
flute
pen

- Using the vocabulary choose and write your own words to recite.
- Clap and recite the chosen words.
- Clap and count out loud: **one, two, three, four.**

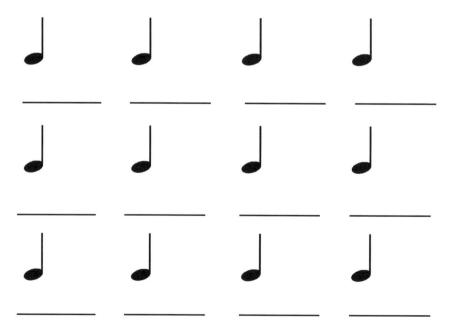

5 Learn to clap and count longer, two syllable words.
Each clap is two counts long.

Pop – corn	Pop – corn	Pop – corn	Pop – corn	one clap = 2 syllables
One – Two	One – Two	One – Two	One – Two	one clap = 2 counts
Pan – cake	Pan – cake	Pan – cake	Pan – cake	
One – Two	One – Two	One – Two	One – Two	
Air – port	Air – plane	Air – port	Air – plane	
One – Two	Three – Four	One – Two	Three – Four	

Clap and recite. One word = one clap.

Tooth-brush,   Tooth-paste,   Tooth-brush,   Tooth-paste.
Rain-bow,   Rain-drop,   Rain-bow,   Rain-drop.

Clap and count. Two counts = one clap.

One – Two,   Three – Four,   One – Two,   Three – Four.

21

7 Practice to clap and count Half Notes.
Each note = one clap. Each note = two counts.

- Clap and recite the words.
- Clap and count out loud: ***one-two, three-four.***

♩	♩	♩	♩
Mon-day,	Tues-day,	Fri-day,	Sun-day.
One – Two,	Three – Four,	One – Two,	Three – Four.

♩ = 2 syllables

♩ = 2 counts

Book-case, Book-shelf, Book-mark, Book-store.
One – Two, Three – Four, One – Two, Three – Four.

White-fish, Fish-hook, Sky-light, Sun-roof.
One – Two, Three – Four, One – Two, Three – Four.

Egg-shell, High-way, Day-light, Week-day.
One – Two, Three – Four, One – Two, Three – Four.

Jack-pot, Rain-coat, Rain-storm, Life-boat.
One – Two, Three – Four, One – Two, Three – Four.

© Victor Shevtsov, 2014

8 Find your own words to recite with Half Notes.
One note = one clap. One note = two counts.

- Clap and recite what you see on the pictures.
- Clap and count out loud: **one-two, three-four.**

Vocabulary

teapot
snowman
footprints
suitcase
starfish
ice-cream
toothbrush
snowflake
rainbow
football
grandson
cheesecake
birthday
moonlight
earthquake
fireworks
skateboard
keyboard
toothpick
saucepan
textbook
postcard
blackbird
blackboard
whitefish
notebook
rainstorm
teaspoon
shoelace
goodbye
bedroom
daylight
schoolboy
sidewalk
watchdog
lifeguard
ballroom

- Using the vocabulary choose and write your own words to recite.
- Clap and recite the chosen words.
- Clap and count out loud: **one, two, three, four.**

24

9 Learn the rhythms with Quarter Notes and Half Notes. Clap each note. **Lively tempo** is recommended (♩ = 112).

♩ = 1 syllable

𝅗𝅥 = 2 syllables

♩ = 1 count

𝅗𝅥 = 2 counts

Snow, Snow, Snow-ball. Rain, Rain, Rain-fall.

One, Two, Three – Four. One, Two, Three – Four.

Snail, Frog, Watch-dog. Cup, Dish, Star-fish.

Sea, Lake, Snow-flake. Pawn, Rook, Fish-hook.

Sheep, Snake, Cheese-cake. Horse, Goat, Rain-coat.

Sun, Moon, Tea-spoon. One, Two, Three – Four.

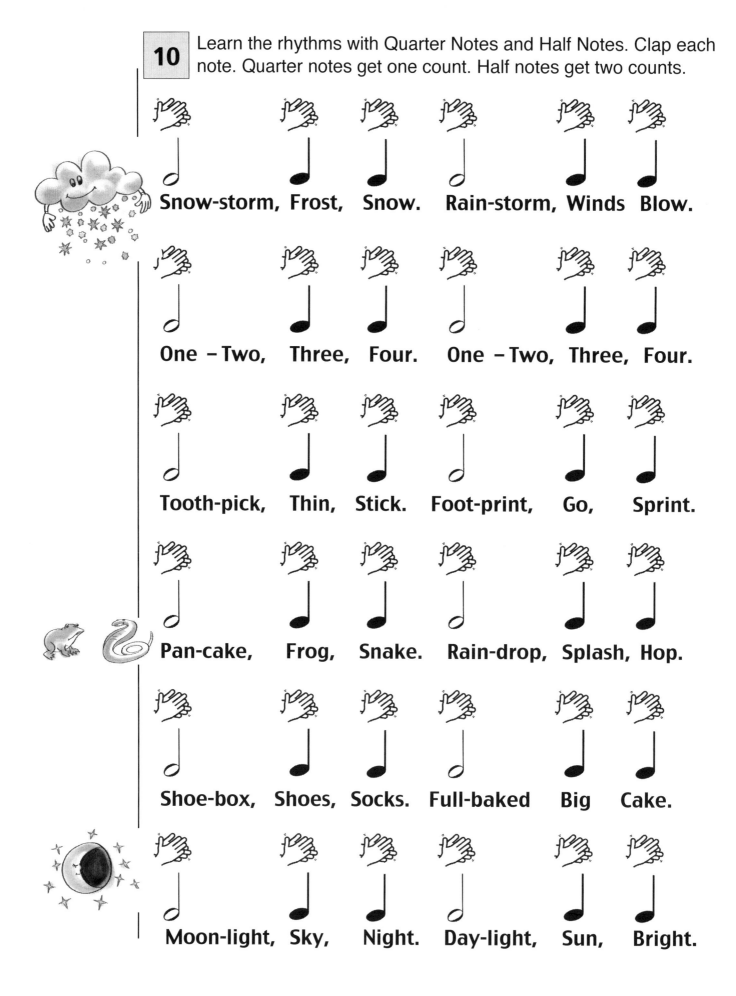

11 Learn the rhythms with Quarter Notes and Half Notes. Clap each note. Quarter notes get one count. Half notes get two counts.

13 Learn to clap and count super long words: one word = four syllables.
Very lively tempo is recommended

Compare **Short Words** to **Super Long Words.**

| Ant | Ant | Ant | Ant | Al – li – ga – tor |

| One | Two | Three | Four | One – Two – Three – Four |

| Snail | Snail | Snail | Snail | Ca – ter – pil – lar |

Do you know any super long words?

| One | Two | Three | Four | One – Two – Three – Four |

| Plum | Plum | Plum | Plum | Wa – ter – me – lon |

| One | Two | Three | Four | One – Two – Three – Four |

Super long sounds are called **Whole Notes**.
We hold them on **four counts** and write like this:

o　　　o　　　o　　　o

14 Learn to clap and count Whole Notes. Each Whole Note is four syllables or four counts long.

o　　　　　　　o
He – li – cop – ter,　One – Two – Three – Four.

o =
4 syllables

o　　　　　　　o
Ex – pla – na – tion,　One – Two – Three – Four.

o =
4 counts

o　　　　　　　o
En – ter – tain – ment,　One – Two – Three – Four.

o　　　　　　　o
Pep – pe – ro – ni,　One – Two – Three – Four.

o　　　　　　　o
Te – le – vi – sion,　One – Two – Three – Four.

15 Rhythmic patterns with Whole Notes and Half Notes.
Whole Note = four counts. Half Note = two counts.

Birth – day,   Birth – day,   Birth – day – par – ty.

One – Two,   Three – Four,   One – Two – Three – Four.

𝐨 = 4 counts

𝅗𝅥 = 2 counts

Soap – dish,   bu – cket,   Su – per – mar – ket.

Sal – ty,   Bit – ter,   Ba – by – sit – ter.

Clap each note.

Soo – ner,   La – ter,   Cal – cu – la – tor.

One – Two,   Three – Four,   One – Two – Three – Four.

© Victor Shevtsov, 2014

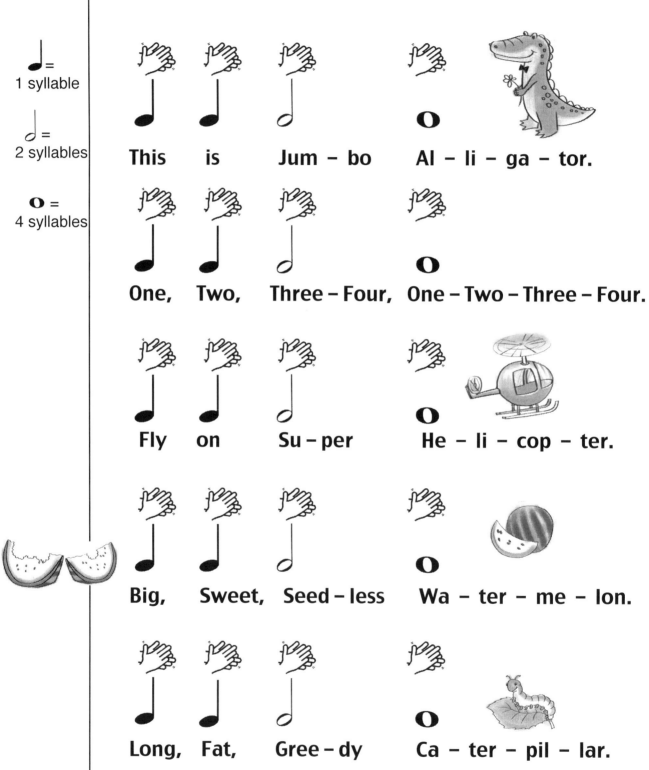

IV. Bars • Bar Lines • Time Signature

Music is always divided into equal parts - **Bars.** This makes reading music easier. You can see the **Bar Lines** separating one bar from another and a **Double Bar Line** at the end of the song.

Usually the bars of the same song are equal. They contain the same number of **beats / counts.** It is like writing a line of words with the same number of syllables.

Each of the following words consists of **four** syllables - beats. Recite and count on your fingers each syllable.

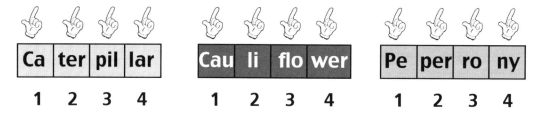

We can put bar lines between equal four syllable words like we put between the music bars.

| 1 | • Recite while counting the syllables on your fingers.
• Number the syllables / beats in each word.
• Put the bar lines after four counts.
• Put the double bar line after each line of words. |

CAL-CU-LA-TOR TE-LE-VI-SION KIN-DER-GAR-TEN

1 2 3 4   _ _ _ _   _ _ _ _

CA-TER-PI-LAR HE-LI-COP-TER BIRTH-DAY-PAR-TY

_ _ _ _   _ _ _ _   _ _ _ _

COM-PE-TI-TION BA-BY-SIT-TER SU-PER-MAR-KET

In the following examples all music bars are equal. They may contain different note values but the number of beats / counts is the same in every bar.

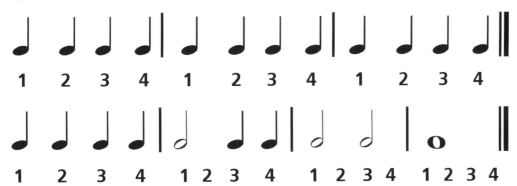

The number at the beginning of the song shows how many beats each bar contains. It is called **Time Signature.**

The Time Signature **4** shows that there are four beats / counts in every bar.

Each of the following words consists of **three** syllables - beats. Recite and count on your fingers each syllable.

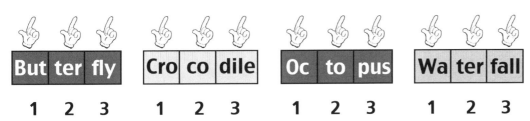

We can put bar lines between equal **three** syllable words like we put between the music bars.

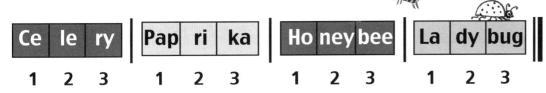

2
- Recite while counting the syllables on your fingers.
- Number the syllables / beats in each word.
- Put the bar lines after four counts.
- Put the double bar line after each line of words.

E-LE-PHANT │ DI-NO-SAUR   STRAW-BER-RY
  1 2 3   — — —   — — —

BUM-BLE-BEE   PO-NY-TAIL   TE-LE-PHONE
  — — —   — — —   — — —

GRASS-HOP-PER   BUT-TER-MILK   CU-CUM-BER
  — — —   — — —   — — —

In the following examples each bar contains three beats. The note values can be different, but the number of beats / counts is the same in every bar.

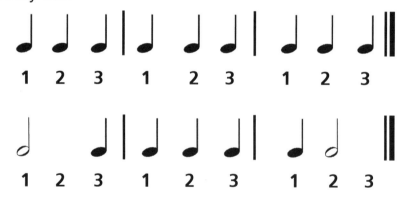

The Time Signature **3** shows that there are three beats / counts in every bar.

- Clap and count the following rhythmic patterns.
- Number the counts - beats.
- Put the bar lines after the fourth count and the double bar line at the end.

V. Note Values • Dotted Half Note

You know already how to clap and count short Quarter Notes, long Half Notes and very long Whole Notes:

In music we also use a Dotted Half Note ♩., which is longer than a Half Note, but shorter than the Whole Note.

A Dotted Half Note is three counts long.

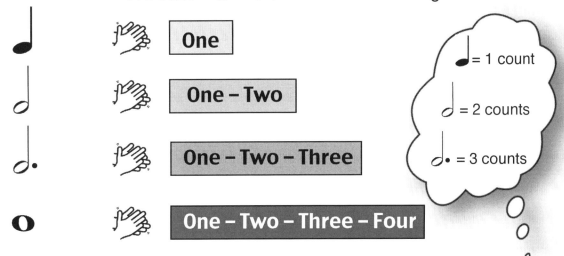

1 Learn to clap Dotted Half Notes. Suggested tempo: ♩=132.

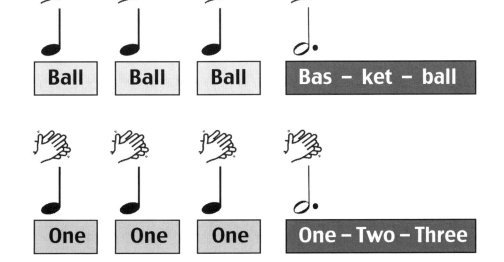

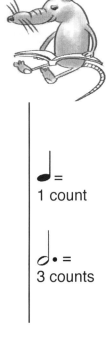

Learn to clap Dotted Half Notes.

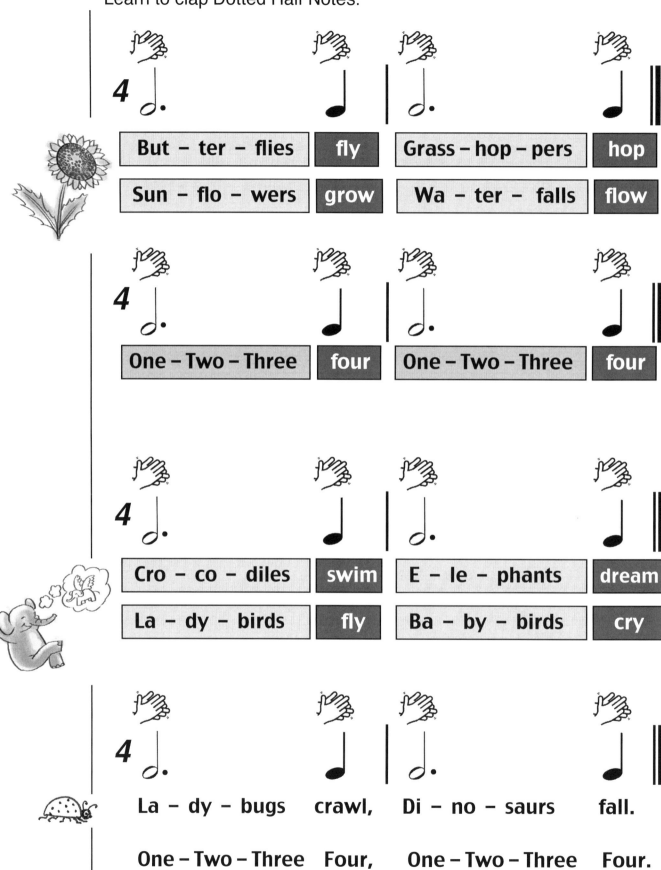

2. Learn to clap and count rhythmic patterns with Dotted Half Note.

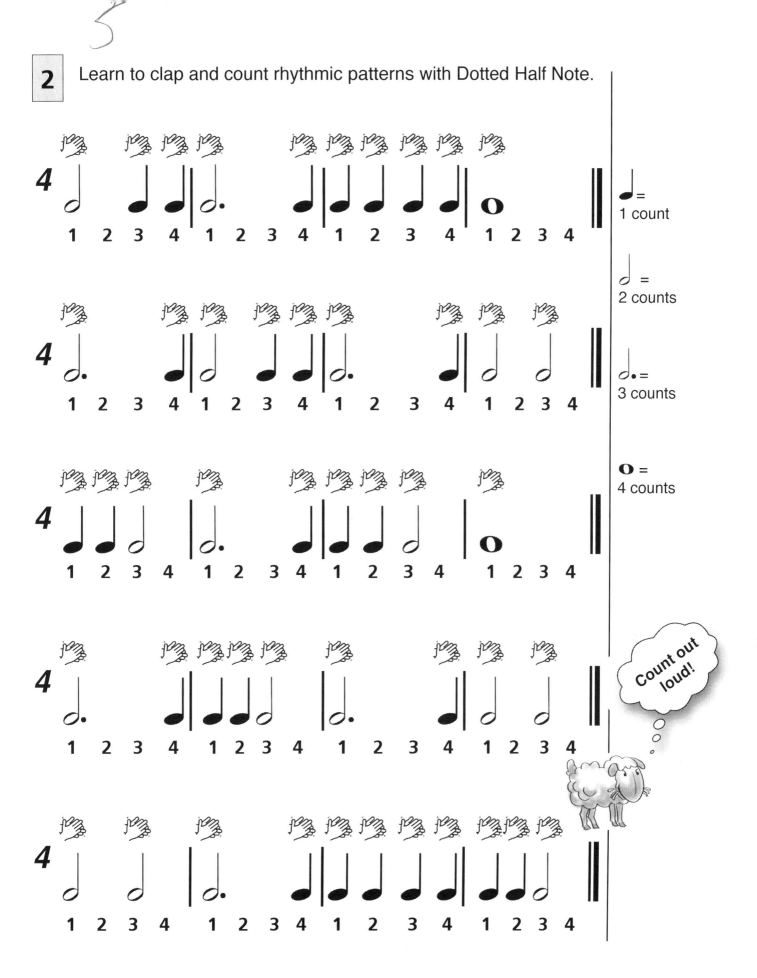

3 Practice to clap and count the following rhythmic patterns.

4 counts in every bar.

♩ = 1 count

𝅗𝅥 = 2 counts

𝅗𝅥. = 3 counts

𝅝 = 4 counts

VI. Rests

A Rest in music is a sign of silence. Rests, like notes, can be short and long. Remember how we write different rests:

Quarter Rest
Silence for
One Beat

Half Rest
Silence for
Two Beats

Whole Rest
Silence for
Four Beats

When you practice to clap rhythmic patterns

clap the **Notes**   do not clap the **Rests**

Examples of rhythms with Rests.

1 Practice these rhythmic exercises. Clap and count.

2 Practice these rhythmic exercises. Clap and count.

3 Practice these rhythmic exercises. Clap and count.

4 Rhythmic exercises to clap and count.

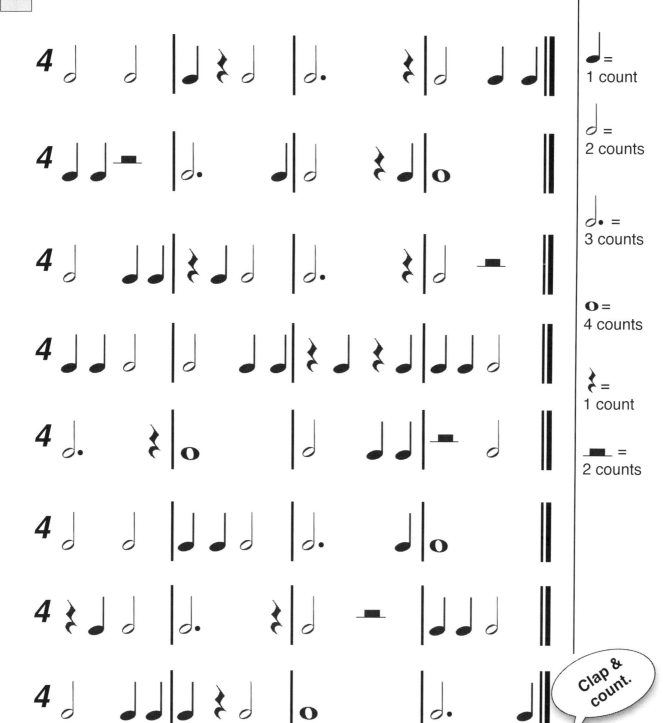

VII. Note Values • Eighth Notes

1 Learn to recite and clap short sounds and **very short sounds**. Clap and recite in a moderately **slow tempo**.

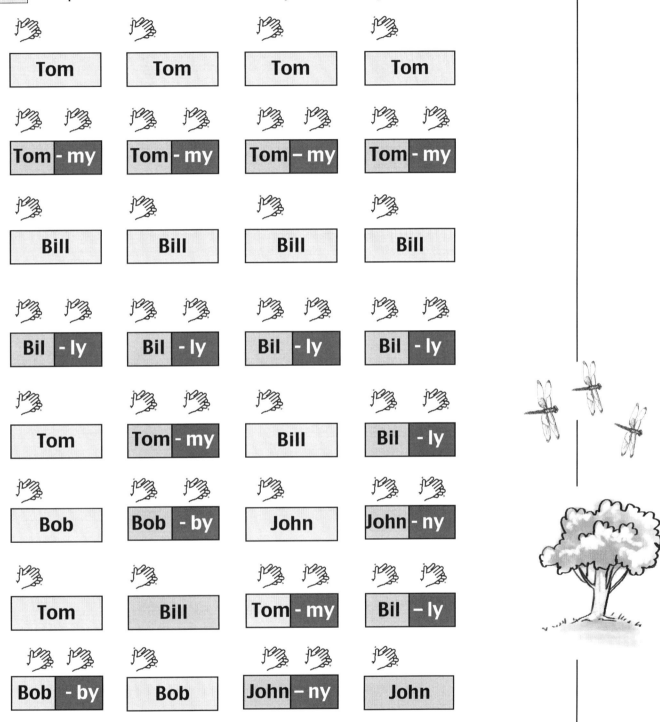

Sounds, which are shorter than Quarter Notes we call **Eighth Notes**. We write Eighth Notes like that:

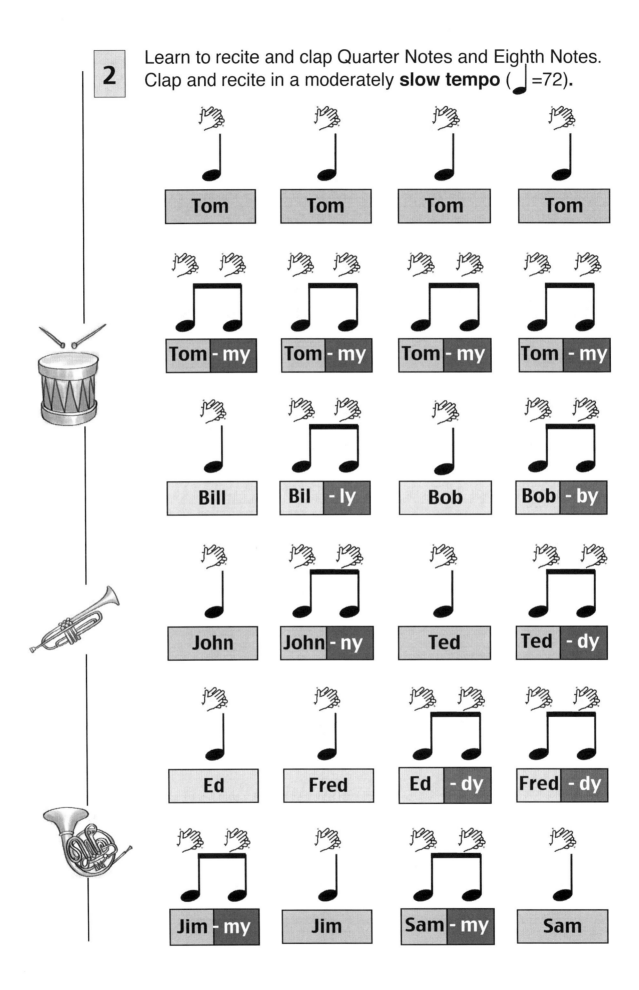

4 When clapping Eighth Notes always count **one - and, two - and, three - and, four - and**. When clapping Quarter Notes, Half Notes and Whole Notes simply count **one, two, three, four**.

Remember: counting **one - and, two - and, three - and, four-and** is twice as fast as counting **one, two, three, four**.

Notice how we clap and count rhythms with different Note Values.

5 Learn to clap and count rhythmic patterns, which contain Quarter Notes and Eighth Notes.

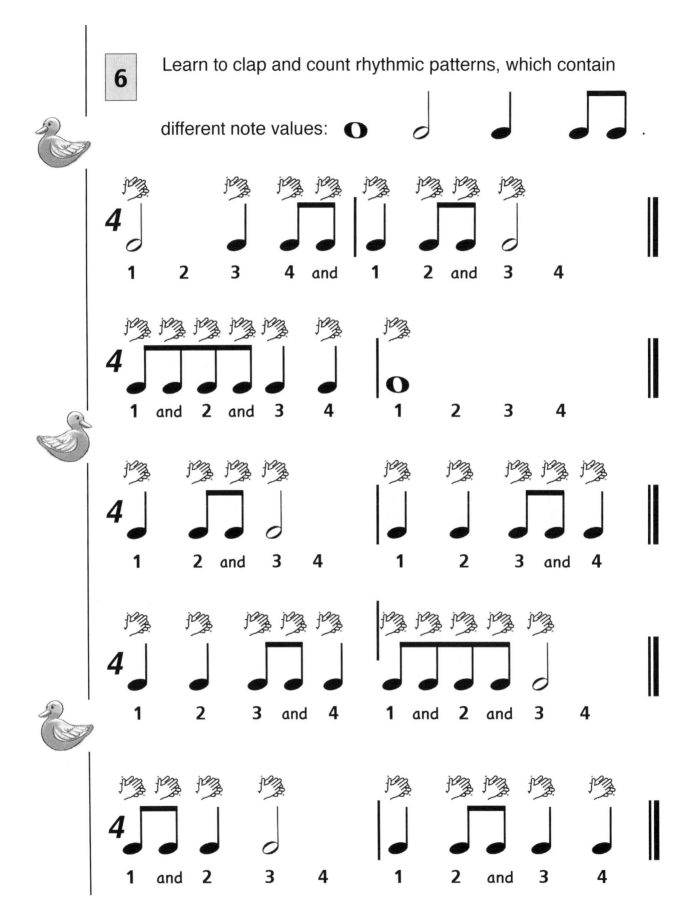

7 Learn to clap and count rhythmic patterns, which contain the following note values:

8 Practice to clap and count the following rhythmic patterns.

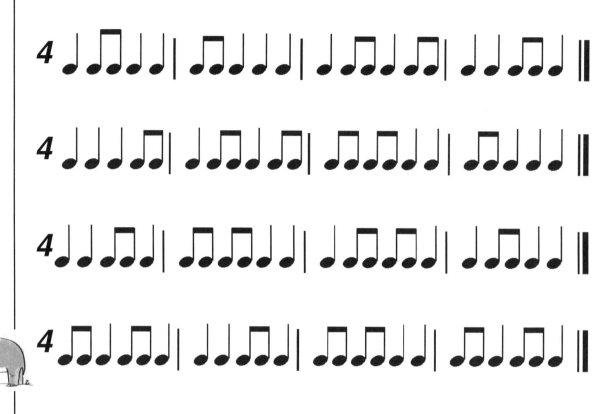

1 quarter note equals 2 eighth notes.

1 = 1 - and

9 Practice to clap and count the following rhythmic patterns.

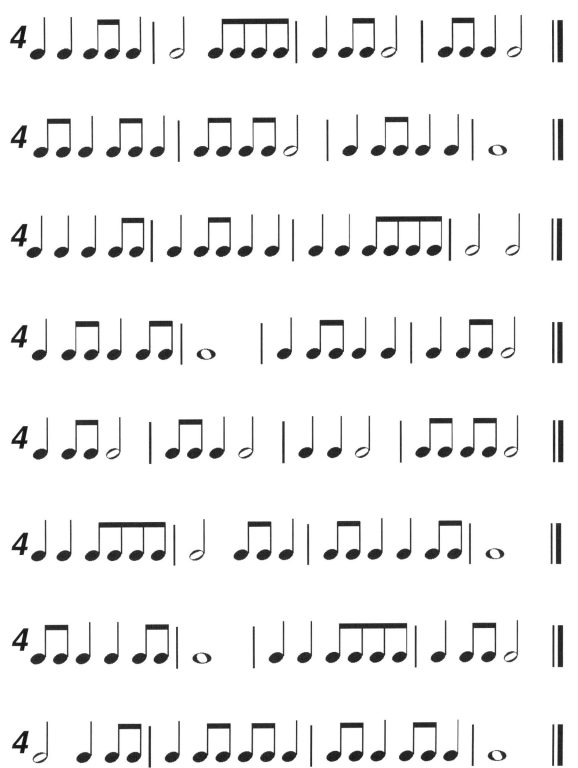

10 Practice to clap and count the following rhythmic patterns.

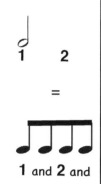

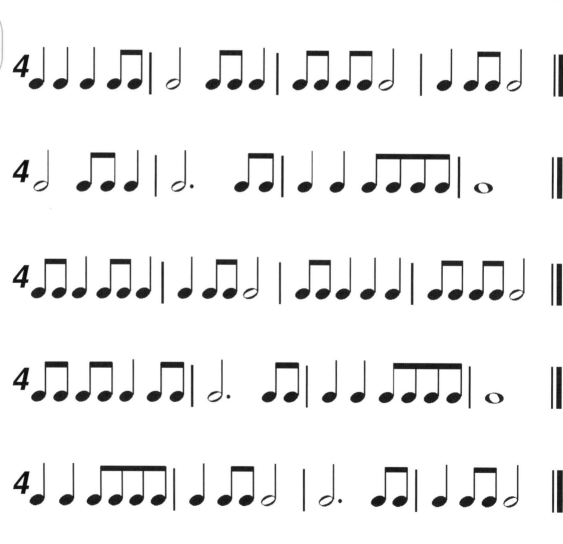

11 Practice to clap and count the following rhythmic patterns.

VIII. Rests • Eighth Rest

1 Rests, which are shorter than the Quarter Rests are called **Eighth Rests.** We write Eighth Rests like that: 𝄾.

Eighth Rest is equal in duration to Eighth Note, but has no sound. A Rest is a sign of silence.

Clap and recite the eighth note rhythm.

Bob – by,   Bob – by,   Tom – my,   Tom – my.

Clap and recite the rhythm with eighth notes and eighth rests. Clap the notes. Do not clap the rests. Recite silently in your mind the silent (grey) part of the word.

Bob – by,   Bob – by,   Tom – my,   Tom – my,

Clap and count the eighth note rhythm.

1 – and   2 – and   3 – and   4 – and

Clap and count the rhythm with eighth notes and eighth rests. Do not clap for the rests. Count silently in your mind the silent part of the rhythm.

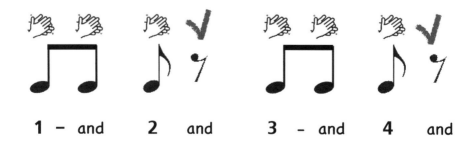

1 – and   2   and   3 – and   4   and

2 Learn to clap and count rhythms with eighth notes and eighth rests.

A rest is a sign of silence.

3 More examples to clap and count. Rhythms with eighth rests.

4 Practice to clap and count rhythms with eighth rests.

5 More examples to clap and count. Rhythms with eighth rests.

6 Practice to clap and count rhythms with eighth rests.

7 More examples to clap and count. Rhythms with eighth rests.

8 Practice to clap and count rhythms with eighth rests.

Practice each rhythm two times.

9

More examples to clap and count. Rhythms with eighth rests.

1 2 and 3 4 and 1 2 3 4 and 1 2 and 3 and 4

1 and 2 3 and 4 1 and 2 and 3 4 1 and 2 and 3 4

 = 2 counts

 = 3 counts

1 and 2 3 4 1 2 3 4 1 and 2 and 3 and 4

1 2 3 4 and 1 2 3 4 and 1 and 2 and 3 4

1 2 and 3 4 and 1 2 3 and 4 and 1 2 3 4

1 and 2 and 3 4 and 1 2 3 and 4 1 2 3 4

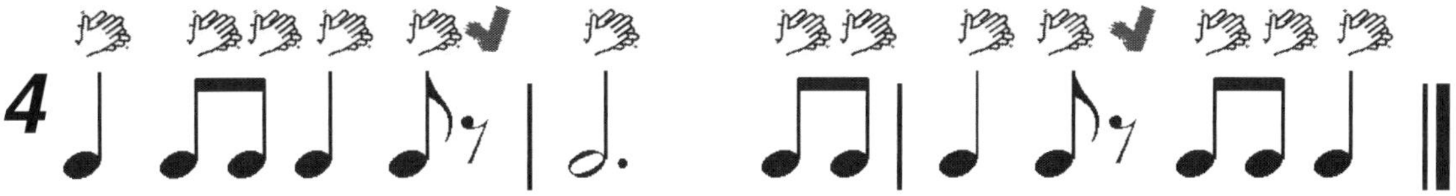

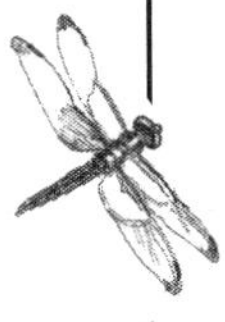

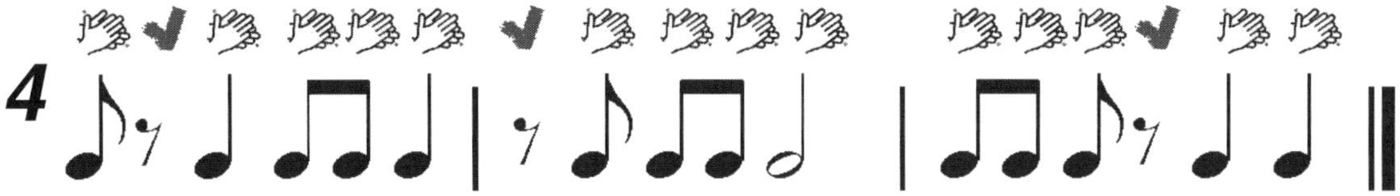

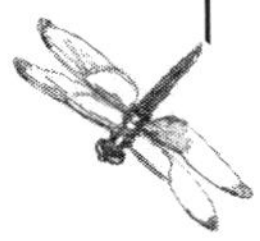

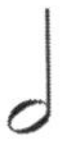

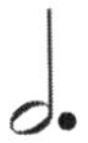

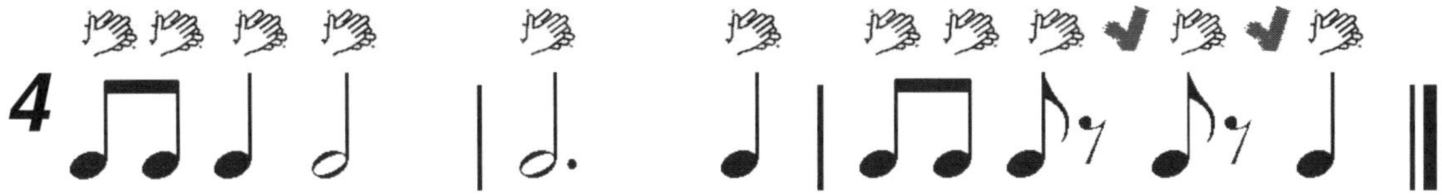

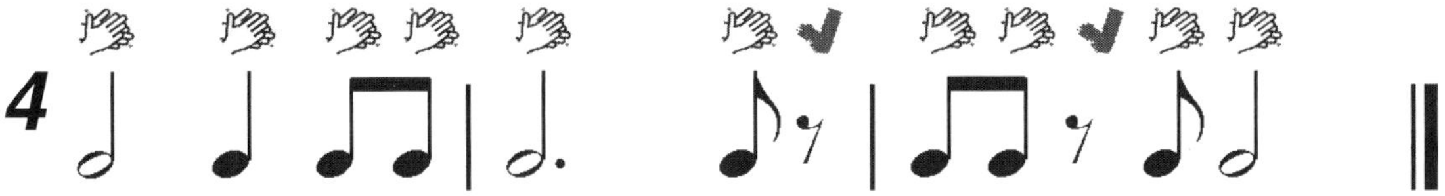

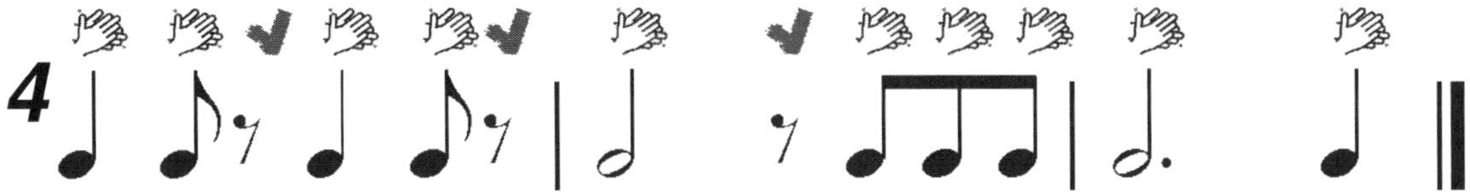

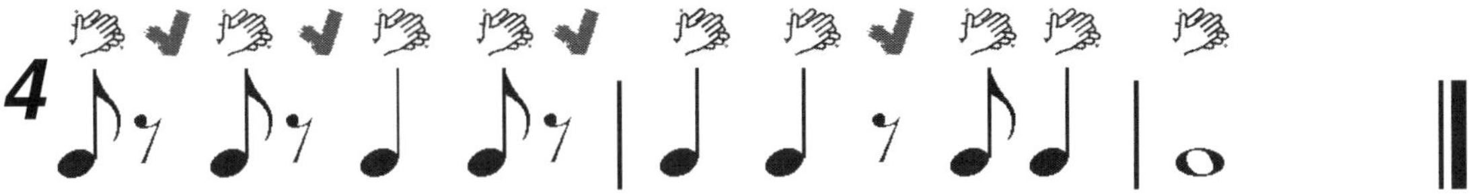

10 Practice to clap and count rhythms with eighth rests.

IX. Overview Exercises

1 Put the bar lines. Make sure that there are 4 beats (counts) in every bar. Put the double bar line at the end of the rhythm.

There should be 4 counts in each bar.

2 Put the bar lines. Make sure that there are 4 beats (counts) in every bar. Remember the time value of rests. Rest should have the same number of counts as notes of the same value.

3 Practice to clap and count the following rhythms.

4 Practice to clap and count the following rhythms.

5 Practice to clap and count the following rhythms.

6 Practice to clap and count the following rhythms.

7 Practice to clap and count the following rhythms.

8 Practice to clap and count the following rhythms.

Made in the USA
San Bernardino, CA
12 August 2014